Our Beautiful Qur'an Journey
Collection of Soul Reflections

by Umm Zakiyyah
and Tadabbur students

Our Beautiful Qur'an Journey:
   Collection of Soul Reflections
by Umm Zakiyyah and Tadabbur students

Tadabbur Authors
Amatullah bint Abdullah
Aminah Hamidullah
Hajara Salihu
Layla Graham
Kameelah Muslimah Kareem
Kathryn Holmes-Adamu
Rasheedah Adisa
Sabah Hassan Abdillahi
Sunny Majeedah
Umm Jameelah
Umm Katheer
Umm Maryam
Umm Zakiyyah
Zarreen Jeri Zowjah-Malik

Copyright © 2021 by Al-Walaa Publications.
All Rights Reserved.

UZ Soul Care info at **uzuniversity.com** and **uzhearthub.com**

Arabic script of Qur'an from corpus.quran.com.
English excerpts from the Qur'an are taken from Saheeh
International, Darussalam, and Yusuf Ali translations of
meanings.

Published by Al-Walaa Publications
Gwynn Oak, Maryland USA

Table of Contents

What Is Tadabbur?

The Arabic term *tadabbur* refers to sincere reflection or contemplation and is taken from the *ayah* in the Qur'an that has been translated to mean: *"Do they not then think deeply on the Qur'an, or are their hearts locked up?"* (Muhammad, 47:24).

The Tadabbur program at Our Beautiful Qur'an Journey is taught by Umm Zakiyyah (along with carefully selected UZ Ambassadors and special guests) and is designed for students of all levels. The women who are selected for Tadabbur are committed to connecting to the Qur'an in a way that nourishes their emotional and spiritual health.

The goal of Tadabbur is to inspire lifetime commitment to Qur'an-centered personal improvement in our daily lives, and at Our Beautiful Qur'an Journey, our Tadabbur program is rooted self-love, self-honesty, and emotional health for the female soul; and the three principles of Tadabbur, as reflection in our weekly journal reflections, are sincerity, humility, and vulnerability.

Find out more at uzhearthub.com.

Preface
Self-Love for the Female Soul

Some time ago, after teaching Qur'an for many years, I cancelled all my classes. I needed some time for myself. I needed time and space to think. I needed to prioritize my own emotional and spiritual health. I also needed to reflect on why I felt that "something was missing" from so many Qur'an programs I'd grown accustomed to over the years.

During this time of self-reflection, I realized that a truly effective Qur'an program needs to be "heart and soul" centered and focused on more than rote memorization of Tajweed rules and recitation of only the words of Qur'an.

It needs to inspire the heart and nourish the soul—and it needs to reflect the beautiful spiritual journey that we are committing to when we study Allah's Book.

It was this realization that inspired Our Beautiful Qur'an Journey, a compassionate program for women offered via uzhearthub.com that supports the female soul on her journey through Tajweed, Hifdh, and Tadabbur.

When I decided to start the program, I told myself: *Even if only one woman joins, I will dedicate my time and resources to supporting her beautiful Qur'an journey, bi'idhnillaah.* At the time that I am writing this preface to our first book, by the mercy of Allah, we are a growing community of more than thirty women from all over the world.

In Our Beautiful Qur'an Journey, we come together to learn, memorize, and reflect on the Dhikr (the divine message and reminder) that Allah revealed as a gift of guidance to mankind till the end of time. He says:

$$\text{إِنَّا نَحْنُ نَزَّلْنَا ٱلذِّكْرَ وَإِنَّا لَهُۥ لَحَـٰفِظُونَ ۝}$$

"Verily We, it is We Who have sent down the Dhikr, and surely, We will guard it [from corruption]."
—*Al-Hijr* (15:9)

Our Merciful Rabb also says:

$$\text{ٱلَّذِينَ ءَامَنُوا۟ وَتَطْمَئِنُّ قُلُوبُهُم بِذِكْرِ ٱللَّهِ أَلَا بِذِكْرِ ٱللَّهِ تَطْمَئِنُّ ٱلْقُلُوبُ ۝}$$

"Those who believe, and whose hearts find rest (and satisfaction) in the remembrance (dhikr) of Allah, for without doubt in the remembrance of Allah do hearts find rest."
—*Ar-Ra'd* (13:28)

It is the latter *ayah* that is at the heart of this book, a collection of soul reflections from the students of Tadabbur, taken from their weekly journals wherein they write a personal reflection on a Surah or ayah of the Qur'an. Each journal reflection is rooted in the three principles of our Tadabbur program: sincerity, humility, and vulnerability.

Additionally, at the heart of each of these reflections is the foundation of our program itself: self-love, self-honesty, and emotional health for the female soul. I pray our reflections touch your heart and inspire you to draw closer to your Merciful Rabb in this world and in the Hereafter.

Sincerely,

Umm Zakiyyah
September 3rd, 2021
26th of Muharram, 1443 AH

For the imperfect, beautiful female soul striving to love herself and never let go of faith in her Merciful Rabb.

أَفَلَا يَتَدَبَّرُونَ ٱلْقُرْءَانَ أَمْ عَلَىٰ قُلُوبٍ أَقْفَالُهَآ ﴿٢٤﴾

—Qur'an (Muhammad, 47:24)

PART ONE
Awakening

1

The Unseen Beauty of Life and Soul
by Umm Zakiyyah

"Alif. Laam. Meem. This is the Book whereof there is no doubt, a guidance to those who are muttaqoon (people of taqwaa), who believe in the ghayb (unseen), establish the Salaah, and spend out of what We have provided for them."
—Al-Baqarah, 2:1-3

I couldn't make it make sense, any of it. Everything I'd assumed about my life, my faith, and the community of Muslims just didn't make sense anymore. My existence as a female soul didn't even make sense anymore. At the time that I was battling this internal confusion, I wasn't just going through a divorce. I was going through spiritual crisis.

Somewhere deep inside, I wanted to be Muslim, but I didn't know *how* to be. I didn't know if there was any place for me. I didn't know if I could ever get it right.

The truth is—and as I write these words, this isn't a feeling I'm particularly proud of—I was beginning to wonder if my Rabb Himself even *wanted* me as part of the ummah. It felt like everywhere I turned, those who claimed to be calling to His path were saying I wasn't on it.

No matter how hard I tried—and Allah knows I tried *hard*—I couldn't dress properly. I couldn't speak properly. I couldn't even *think* properly, particularly in the context of striving to be a good Muslim wife. "If you were truly a righteous woman," a man told me once, "then you wouldn't even have *thoughts* that disagree with your husband, even if you submit to his decision in the end."

Then there were those things that my Creator had decreed for me that were completely out of my control— like my skin color, my gender, and my American background. Yet all of these things were consistently treated as if they reflected some inherent flaw or sin within me.

And even amongst those things that were within my control, mentally and emotionally, I was losing the strength to keep up. It was all becoming so suffocating and overwhelming: the things that were expected of me, the things that were demanded of me, and the things that were being taken from me.

It feels like no matter how small I shrink myself, I wrote in my journal, *I'm never small enough.*

Naturally, all of this internal overwhelm affected my worship, as well as my spiritual connection to my faith and my Creator. Salaah became tremendously difficult for me, and during this difficult time, I would often crawl to prayer and pray sitting down, I was so weak and depressed.

But I prayed.

And though I wasn't particularly motivated to read the Qur'an each day as had been my habit for years, I continued to read and recite from Allah's Book—even if I could muster only enough strength to read a single *ayah* or a couple of lines.

The truth is, despite everything that I was going through, reciting the Qur'an gave my heart comfort, and I didn't want to go a single day without it soothing my hurting heart. Moreover, it terrified me to think of the possibility of abandoning the Qur'an so much that Allah would remove from me my ability to recite with Tajweed and understand the Arabic.

Not only that. Deep down, I also hoped that this dark time would pass and I could find my way back to my Merciful Rabb somehow.

But I didn't see how.

I was even beginning to wonder if I'd misunderstood Islam itself all these years. Looking at the state of the Muslims and how so many mistreated women, Black people, and Americans and then used the *deen* itself to justify it, I began to ask myself, *Is it possible this is actually the deen? Is it possible that within the Qur'an itself was actual justification for this?*

I began to battle these doubts daily.

"This is the Book whereof there is no doubt…" I read in the Qur'an during this time.

But what about all these people using Allah's Book to harm and mistreat others? I wondered. How was it even possible that these people were rightly guided?

*"…a guidance to those who are *muttaqoon* (people of taqwaa)."*

It was at these words that my heart momentarily stopped, and my mind became alert to a message that I'd never comprehended before: This Book is a source of guidance to only the people who have *taqwaa*—not to those who are merely "Muslim."

SubhaanAllah.

You see, in the Qur'an and prophetic teachings, *taqwaa* refers to sincere and humble consciousness of the Creator that inspires daily soul care that protects you from committing any *dhulm* (oppression, abuse, mistreatment, or wronging the self or others)—except that you immediately repent, correct yourself, and redress any wrongs you've done to someone else.

In this way, *taqwaa* is a spiritual practice that consistently protects your soul from spiritual harm in this world and from any cause for being punished in the Hereafter.

"This is the Book whereof there is no doubt, a guidance to the people of taqwaa…"

The words brought so much clarity to me, and I started to feel the doubts about my faith leaving bit by bit. But I still didn't know how to move forward with so much religious corruption and mistreatment all around me. Where do I even begin finding my place amongst people who claimed to share my faith but showed so little care and respect for me?

I had no idea. But still, I asked Allah to write me down amongst the people of *taqwaa*. I just couldn't imagine where I would even begin walking this path though, my heart was so broken spiritually.

"…[those] who believe in the ghayb (unseen)."

In that moment, these divine words hit my heart in a way they never had before, and it was as if my heart was saying to me: *Before this moment, you used to think of believing in the ghayb as only about believing in the unseen as it relates to concepts like Allah and His angels, or Paradise and Hellfire. But today, from this moment forward, as you strive upon taqwaa, you're going to have to believe in the unseen as it relates to the khayr (the spiritual goodness) of this ummah today, though your eyes do not see it and your mind does not perceive it. This is what it will mean for you to be amongst those who are guided by the Qur'an, whereof there is no doubt, and written down amongst the people of taqwaa—the only people who will truly experience and live by its merciful teachings.*

Tears came to my eyes as I realized from the depths of my heart that my Merciful Rabb was showing me the way back to Him.

Through believing in the unseen beauty of my life and soul.

I just needed to hold onto my faith, keep up with my Salaah, and to be generous with the gifts and provision Allah had given me.

"…the people of taqwaa, [those] who believe in the ghayb, establish the Salaah, and spend out of what We have provided for them."

O Allah, make me amongst them!

2

Where Do I Fit In?
by Umm Jameelah

*"[O Allah! Guide me upon] the path of those upon whom You have
bestowed favor, not of those who have evoked [Your] anger, or of those
who have gone astray."*
—Al-Faatihah, 1:7

SubhanAllaaah! Two paths. Actually three. Where do I
fit in? Grace? Anger? Be honest with yourself. Where
are you with Allah? What path do you want to take?
Truly? A lot of questions, no definite answer. I am soiled
with life. I've let it get the best of me. I've played around
with time. Watching unnecessary things. Being lazy. Not
trying to improve while I know I can.

I'm afraid of the unknown as well. What does wanting
good feel like? Outwardly, I'm pretty positive, hoping I feel
the goodness I'm protruding. Sometimes it's there,
sometimes it's not. My bleeding heart. Rusted. Possibly
sealed. *O Allah, aid me and help me back to you. Ameen.*

Do I aspire for goodness for my hereafter and a good
standing with Allah? For real, sometimes I wonder if I even
truly care because each cut is way too deep, and the aid lies
right before my eyes. *O Allah, put me on your path of grace and*

keep me away from your anger and the path of the people and the jinn. Ameen!

But then again, I'm human and my feelings switch every day.

I want grace.

I want grace.

I want Allah.

3

Taqwaa, the Sweetness of Emaan
by Hajara Salihu

ٱلَّذِينَ يُؤْمِنُونَ بِٱلْغَيْبِ وَيُقِيمُونَ ٱلصَّلَوٰةَ وَمِمَّا رَزَقْنَٰهُمْ يُنفِقُونَ ﴿٣﴾

وَٱلَّذِينَ يُؤْمِنُونَ بِمَآ أُنزِلَ إِلَيْكَ وَمَآ أُنزِلَ مِن قَبْلِكَ وَبِٱلْءَاخِرَةِ هُمْ يُوقِنُونَ ﴿٤﴾

"[The people of taqwaa are those] who believe in the ghayb (unseen), establish the Salaah, and spend out of what We have provided for them. And [they are those] who believe in what has been revealed to you [O Muhammad], and what was revealed before you, and of the Hereafter they are certain [in faith]."
—Al-Baqarah, 2:3-4

Taqwaa. Having *taqwaa* is the sweetness of *emaan*. If I live my life in accordance with the verses above, it flows into me and I am unbothered about my worries and grief because Allah is Al-Baseer (All-Seeing) and Al-Aleem (All-Knowing).

These verses remind me to take stock of my deeds and make *tawbah*, to take responsibility for my actions and be hopeful of Allah's mercy.

In any situation I find myself in, I need to believe in the certainty that Allah will come through for me just as He (Allah) made fire cool and safe for Ibrahim (Abraham, peace be upon him) and split the sea for Musa (Moses, peace be upon him).

I may not be able to see what lies ahead for me, but I have to believe in the unseen and know that Allah is Ar-Raqeeb, the Ever-Watchful.

O Allah, I am in total submission to Your will. I have believed in Your Prophet and Messenger Muhammad (peace be upon him). Yaa Rabb, write me amongst Your believing servants who are upon the right guidance and successful.

4

I Didn't Know
by Kathryn Holmes-Adamu

إِنَّا جَعَلْنَا مَا عَلَى ٱلْأَرْضِ زِينَةً لَّهَا لِنَبْلُوَهُمْ أَيُّهُمْ أَحْسَنُ عَمَلًا ۝

*"Indeed, We have made that which is on the earth a zeenah
(beautification and adornment) for it so that We may test them [as to]
which of them is best in deed."*
—Al-Kahf, 18:7

I didn't know.
What didn't I know?
I didn't know the answer.
I didn't know the answer to the question of why.
What question of why?
The answer for why HE created the adornments.
What adornments?
The adornment of wealth for those who have it.
The adornment of beauty for those who have it.
The adornment of knowledge for those who have it.
The adornment of good health for those who have it.
The adornments of status, education and position for all of
those who have it.
But, as they say, "nothing is truly free".
The answer for why HE created adornments is because it is
a test, you see.

I didn't know that the why is to see who among us is best in deed.

So even if your relative, friend, or anyone else is blessed with uncountable adornments, just remember, each and every one of them is just that - a test.

A test or tests for you and me.

5

The Reality of This World
by Sabah Hassan Abdillahi

لِّكَيْلَا تَأْسَوْا عَلَىٰ مَا فَاتَكُمْ وَلَا تَفْرَحُوا بِمَا آتَاكُمْ وَٱللَّهُ لَا يُحِبُّ كُلَّ مُخْتَالٍ فَخُورٍ ۝

"In order that you may not grieve at the things that you fail to get, nor rejoice over that which has been given to you…"
—Al-Hadeed, 57:23

As humans we consciously and subconsciously chase the adornment of this life, and we tend to get distracted by it. This distraction does not only make us forget the difficulties and the temporary happiness of any journey, but it can also make us become heedless of the fact that we are even on a journey treading the path to our real home, where we originally came from, the everlasting bliss. Once we become heedless of the journey, we also lose focus of the path to the right destination.

A believer focuses on his journey without being distracted by the beauty he may encounter on path and without being confused or frustrated by a loss of any blessing that he attains on the path.

With the help of Allah, may we always be conscious and mindful of our journey so we don't become diverted from our path home: Paradise.

6

Light Upon Light
by Hajara Salihu

۞ ٱللَّهُ نُورُ ٱلسَّمَٰوَٰتِ وَٱلۡأَرۡضِۚ مَثَلُ نُورِهِۦ كَمِشۡكَوٰةٍ فِيهَا مِصۡبَاحٌۖ ٱلۡمِصۡبَاحُ فِى زُجَاجَةٍ ٱلزُّجَاجَةُ كَأَنَّهَا كَوۡكَبٌ دُرِّيٌّ يُوقَدُ مِن شَجَرَةٍ مُّبَٰرَكَةٍ زَيۡتُونَةٍ لَّا شَرۡقِيَّةٍ وَلَا غَرۡبِيَّةٍ يَكَادُ زَيۡتُهَا يُضِىٓءُ وَلَوۡ لَمۡ تَمۡسَسۡهُ نَارٌۚ نُّورٌ عَلَىٰ نُورٍۚ يَهۡدِى ٱللَّهُ لِنُورِهِۦ مَن يَشَآءُۚ وَيَضۡرِبُ ٱللَّهُ ٱلۡأَمۡثَٰلَ لِلنَّاسِۗ وَٱللَّهُ بِكُلِّ شَىۡءٍ عَلِيمٌ ﴿٣٥﴾

*"Allah is the Light of the heavens and the earth.
The example of His light is like a niche within which
is a Lamp, the Lamp is within glass, the glass as if it
were a pearly [white] star lit from [the oil of] of a
blessed olive tree, neither of the east nor of the
west, whose oil would almost glow even if untouched
by fire. Light upon light. Allah guides to His light whom He
wills. And Allah presents examples for the people, and Allah
is Knowing of all things."*
—*An-Noor, 24:35*

I say I am in a dark place. That I am going through this phase of darkness. I am oblivious of the light that surrounds me. The light within me, the one that fills me. The light that has led me to this "dark place."

How quickly I forget the light placed in my heart. And I allow my trials to lower the wick. I complain of my challenges, my struggles, my grief, distress and anxiety.
Has Allah not taught me that He is the Light of the Heavens and the earth?
That even when the wick is low, the Qur'an will spring it up?
That my faith in the unseen and certainty of His mercy will bring me afloat and banish all my worries?
That if I ride the tide despite the darkness and hardships, I'll get ashore and shine like a pearly star lit from the oil of a blessed olive tree.

That is my Rabb!
Light upon light.
He will guide me right
He has led me here and
Will see me through.

My *du'aa* from the Qur'an: *"Our Lord, perfect for us our light and forgive us. Indeed, You are over all things competent"* (66:8).

Yaa Allah, let Your light fill our hearts
Let Your light go before us
Keep shining while we are gone
Let us be known for the light we brought to others
Let this light be our companion until the Day we meet Whom through whose light we have traversed this life.

7

Something Was Missing Inside Me
by Umm Maryam

إِيَّاكَ نَعْبُدُ وَإِيَّاكَ نَسْتَعِينُ ۝

*"[O Allah] You [alone] we worship and You [alone] we ask for aid
and help."*
—*Al-Faatihah*, 1:5

This particular verse from the opening chapter weighs
a lot in my life.

Alhamdulillah, I was blessed to be born in a Muslim
household. As a child, I was taught to worship Allah alone
and ask Him alone for anything and everything.

Every time I read this verse, I had a sense of satisfaction
in my heart that I don't take idols as worship. I don't turn
to people in the graves or saints for worshipping. I used to
be very happy in my bubble that I worship Allah alone.

I reached a point in my life where I accomplished a few
things but there was some void, something missing, and
there began my journey to pursue it—and I found it in one
particular relationship, so again my happiness knew no
bounds.

Until one day that thing was taken away.

It shook my entire world to the core because up until
then, the concept of things being taken away didn't exist in

my mini-world. After all, I always got what I wanted, so when it happened, I couldn't fathom the fact that Allah has the power to take things away whenever He wants.

It was a very short-lived experience, and things had ended abruptly, leaving me devastated.

It was in that period of grief, I reflected on this verse and an entirely different world opened up for me. I stumbled upon the verse from Al-Qur'an in Surah Al-Furqan (25:43):

أَرَءَيْتَ مَنِ ٱتَّخَذَ إِلَٰهَهُ هَوَىٰهُ أَفَأَنتَ تَكُونُ عَلَيْهِ وَكِيلًا ٤٣

"Have you seen the one who takes as his ilah [object of worship] his own vain desire?"

It hit me hard. It answered all my pains and suffering. I had turned away from the remembrance of Allah and hence the depression as mentioned in the Qur'an in Surah Ta Ha (20:124):

وَمَنْ أَعْرَضَ عَن ذِكْرِى فَإِنَّ لَهُ مَعِيشَةً ضَنكًا وَنَحْشُرُهُ يَوْمَ ٱلْقِيَٰمَةِ أَعْمَىٰ

"And whoever turns away from My remembrance - indeed, he will have a depressed life…"

Once when ruminating, I was shocked to realise one such episode of my heart literally bowing to this object of passion. This realization crumbled me even more that I did not stay true to my words in every Salaah, when I said:

"You alone we worship and You alone we ask for help."

O Allah, forgive my sins and shortcomings. O Turner of the hearts, keep our hearts firm on Your religion. Ameen.

8

The Sickness of Envy
by Sabah Hassan Abdillahi

"And [I seek refuge] from the evil of the envious one when he envies."
—Al-Falaq, 113:5

*H*asad or envy, the root cause of *sihr* and the first crime ever committed, is a serious issue. It was the first crime in the heavens, committed by Iblis when he caused our father to eat from the tree, and it was the first crime on earth committed by Qabil (Cain) when he killed his brother Habil (Abel).

A person who has been affected by the action of the envier can fully understand the agony and heartache especially when those enviers are supposed to be the ones protecting him.

A heart that is blackened by the sickness of envy would submit to the command of the devil and is capable of any evil. Such people with this sickness have no limits. They could even envy and harm the poor for merely being content and patient. They could even envy and harm their closest relative in a way one may not even harm his worst enemy. They may even do actions that could take them out of the fold of Islam.

All praise is to Allah for not leaving us on our own, but gifting us with this Surah as well as Surah An-Naas and Al-Iklaas as a protection from the evil of the envier when he envies and acts upon his envy. From His *hikmah*, these are the easiest and shortest *suwar* and the first Sūrahs we ever learn.

As our beloved Prophet (peace be upon him) did:

1. Read these Surahs three times in the morning and three times in the evening
2. Read them after every prayer.
3. Read them three times when going to bed.

The more we read, the more we show Allah that we are in need of Him.

We need to read it more than we need food and water.

9

Finding My Way Back, a Haiku
by Sunny Majeedah

۞ قُلْ يَـٰعِبَادِىَ ٱلَّذِينَ أَسْرَفُوا۟ عَلَىٰٓ أَنفُسِهِمْ لَا تَقْنَطُوا۟ مِن رَّحْمَةِ ٱللَّهِ إِنَّ ٱللَّهَ يَغْفِرُ ٱلذُّنُوبَ جَمِيعًا إِنَّهُۥ هُوَ ٱلْغَفُورُ ٱلرَّحِيمُ ۝

"Say: O My slaves who have wronged their souls! Despair not of the mercy of Allah, verily Allah forgives all sins. Truly, He is the Oft-Forgiving, Most Merciful."
—Az-Zumar 39:53

Finding my way back
After betraying my soul
Hard fought victory

He called me, my soul
Never despair His Mercy
He forgives. Can I?!

Will I forgive me?
Let them pin me to my sins or;
Let them plant my sins to grow
I'll plant a new seed

He is Al-Wadood

So, I love me. I'm human
Loving submission

He is Al-Ghafoor
I forgive myself and them
Still I move with grace

He is Al-Afuw
He erased my faults, turned them good
Like no one else would

His Light is An-Noor
Dark paths lit by my worship
Steps toward success

Coming back is hard
Never leaving is harder
Just don't leave for good

Pray your way back, now!
He's All Hearing, One who guides
Cherish your way back

PART TWO
Accountability

10

The Provision of the Pen
by Umm Zakiyyah

"*…and who believe in the ghayb (unseen), establish prayer, and spend out of what We have provided for them.*"
—*Al-Baqarah*, 2:3

In the first chapter, I reflected on how the Words of my Merciful Rabb awakened my heart when they spoke of the *ghayb*, the unseen. So, let me now share a time when the Words of my Merciful Rabb awakened my heart when they spoke of the seen—a reality and experience well-known to my heart and soul.

I must have been only ten years old. I don't remember my exact age, but I remember I was quite young. I recall sitting alongside my sisters and brothers on the carpet of the living room floor after Fajr, the dawn prayer, as my father read to us from the Qur'an, as was the daily custom in our home.

This particular day he was reading the opening verses from Surah Al-Baqarah, which have been translated to mean:

"Alif. Laam. Meem. This is the Book whereof there is no doubt, a guidance to those who are muttaqoon (people of taqwaa), who believe

in the ghayb (unseen), establish the Salaah, and spend out of what We have provided for them" (2:1-3).

I'd heard these *ayaat* before, but for some reason, my young heart became alert to them as it never had before. In that moment, my heart became humble in submission as these profound words settled into it: *"…and [who] spend out of what We have provided for them"* (2:3).

Right then, it was as if my *nafs* was saying to me: *Allah provided you with the gift of the pen, so it is your responsibility to spend of this provision for His sake. So, use your gift of writing to remind people of Him. And remember, dear soul, you will be held accountable for how you spend from the wealth of talents that your Merciful Rabb has given you.*

11

Walk Away from Harming Your Soul
by Zarreen Jeri Zowjah-Malik

أَفَرَءَيْتَ مَنِ ٱتَّخَذَ إِلَٰهَهُ هَوَىٰهُ وَأَضَلَّهُ ٱللَّهُ عَلَىٰ عِلْمٍ وَخَتَمَ عَلَىٰ سَمْعِهِ وَقَلْبِهِ وَجَعَلَ عَلَىٰ بَصَرِهِ غِشَٰوَةً فَمَن يَهْدِيهِ مِنۢ بَعْدِ ٱللَّهِ أَفَلَا تَذَكَّرُونَ ﴿٢٣﴾

"Have you seen he who has taken as his ilah (object of worship) his [own vain] desire, and Allah has sent him astray due to knowledge and has set a seal upon his hearing and his heart and put over his vision a veil? So who will guide him after Allah? Then will you not be reminded?"
—*Al-Jaathiyah* (45:23)

*B*ismillah.
Then will you not be reminded? Then will I not be reminded?
...*InshaaAllah.*

I pray that I, my family, my friends, my community, and the Ummah will *not* be set astray due to KNOWLEDGE and set a seal upon our hearing and our heart and put over our vision a veil. *Ameen...*

I pray that I am always reminded through all good-times and difficulties to follow the Quran and Sunnah. *Ameen.*

I pray that my "worldly knowledge" and pride *don't* lead to my heart becoming veiled!

Ameen.
Please, don't let me disregard my Lord, Allah (*subhaanahu wa ta'alaa, Glorified and High is He!*)
Ameen!

In this dunya, it's a constant drag-out, pull-down, hair-pulling, fistfight to stay on the straight path and FOLLOW the guidance sent by Allah (*subhaanahu wa ta'alaa*). Surrounded by the *haraam*, it can become mundane.

Can't let it become mundane and therefore *accept* the evil whisperings. The evil whisper is real. Not only into your ear, but your sight, your hands, and your feet can be compelled to respond to the evil whispers.
Then if I do, I worry about whether I can repent soon enough, and to always acknowledge the evil whisperings, and turn away as soon as possible.

May Allah (subhaanahu wa ta'alaa, Glorified and High is He!) forgive me.

I often cry.

Knowing my ears and eyes are listening and seeing, on the daily, mundane and *haraam* everywhere. It often seems unavoidable. Though you start with so-called "safe *dunya* material," where you are less likely to be exposed to the *haraam*, you self-censor for the sake of your soul.

Yet still, reading for pleasure, here it comes again…
May Allah (subhaanahu wa ta'alaa, Glorified and High is He!) forgive me.
Looking up twice, riding down the street…
May Allah (subhaanahu wa ta'alaa, Glorified and High is He!) forgive me.
Watching "family entertainment"…
May Allah (subhaanahu wa ta'alaa, Glorified and High is He!) forgive me.
Putting on that outfit, a tiny bit too tight…

May Allah (subhaanahu wa ta'alaa, Glorified and High is He!) forgive me.
Staying in the gossiping crowd too long…
May Allah (subhaanahu wa ta'alaa, Glorified and High is He!) forgive me.

For each and every one of these *haraam* moments, may I always recognize them and ask for forgiveness and fast-forward, turn down the volume on that part, turn my eyes away, donate those clothes, and walk away.

For this is a way of life for those who know not to trust their "worldly intellect," always flawed and ever-changing, but instead hold on to the STRONG rope of Allah (*subhaanahu wa ta'alaa*) and trust in Allah's guidance and act upon His reminders.

For He is the Righteous Teacher.

12

Consciousness of Allah
by Sabah Hassan Abdillahi

ذَٰلِكَ ٱلْكِتَٰبُ لَا رَيْبَ فِيهِ هُدًى لِّلْمُتَّقِينَ ﴿٢﴾

"This is the Book whereof there is no doubt, a guidance to those who have taqwaa."
—*Al-Baqarah, 2:2*

Having *taqwaa* (consciousness of Allah) is creating a barrier between myself and the punishment of Allah. Being conscious of my relationship with Allah should mean that I do that which He is pleased with and avoid that which displeases Him.

The sweetness and beauty of having *taqwaa* is that it would lead to having true self-care, not what self-care looks like today and what it looked like to me—as the hot baths and yoga which is mainly focus on the external. But true self-care is the inward self-care which is giving time to that which nourishes the soul, such as *'ebaadah, dhikr,* and protecting the soul from all that which is harmful, such as sins.

Furthermore, having *taqwaa* would lead to being more conscious of how to deal with others; such as making excuses for others.

Moreover, *taqwaa* is in the heart, and the heart is the vehicle for reflecting on the Qur'an. Striving to continuously have *taqwaa* should increase my relationship with the Qur'an. Hence the *ayah* ends with "…a guidance to those who have *taqwaa*."

In other words, having *taqwaa* should:

1. Better my relationship with Allah.
2. Better my relationship with His revelation.
3. Better my relationship with myself.
4. Better my relationship with others.

13

Allow the Qur'an To Complete You
by Layla Graham

"…and recite the Qur'an with measured recitation."
—*Al-Muzzammil, 73:4*

For years, my main Qur'an objective during Ramadan was to finish at least one, if not more, *khatm* (completion) of the entire Qur'an. We know the virtues of reading the entire Qur'an. Every year at the end of Ramadan, we crowd the *masaajid* so we can be part of that *khitmah* (the completion of the Qur'an) and that *du'aa mustajab* (accepted supplication).

This is not about diminishing the importance and the virtue of completing a reading of the Qur'an.

This is to remind the believers in Allah and The Last Day that Al-Qur'an first and foremost is our guide because it is the Word of God. Reading and reciting Al-Qur'an without taking the time to contemplate on the words and reflect upon them is doing a great injustice to yourself.

Allow Al-Qur'an to complete you.
Allow Al-Qur'an to comfort you.
Allow Al-Qur'an to warn you.
Allow Al-Qur'an to teach you.
Allow Al-Qur'an to remind you.

Allow Al-Qur'an to consume you.
Allow Al Qur'an to guide you.

Can you hear Allah speaking to you through your own voice as you recite His Words? Can you hear Him reprimanding you, or praising you, or giving you glad tidings?

He is our RABB. Allah disciplines us through His revelation. Allah provides us with countless examples and analogies so that we, the people of intellect, could understand and reflect, and apply it to our lives and our world.

O Allah, grant us mercy through Al-Qur'an, and allow it to be our leader, our light, our guide, and our mercy.
Yaa Allah, remind us of Al-Qur'an what we may have forgotten, and teach us of Al-Qur'an what we are ignorant of, and grant us the rizq of reciting Al-Qur'an in the depths of the night, and in the peaks of the day.
O Allah, cause the Qur'an to be a case for us on the Day of Judgement, O Lord of all creation!

14

Fear Hypocrisy, Dear Soul
by Sabah Hassan Abdillahi

*"And of the people are some who say, 'We believe in Allah and the
Last Day,' but they are not [really] believers."*
—Al-Baqarah, 2:8

As a protection and fear of resembling such people,
rushing to the obedience of Allah, especially when
I am alone and only Allah can see me, would allow
me to sincerely confirm my belief in Allah and the Last
Day.

These verses about the hypocrites remind me of how
afraid the leaders and earliest generations of this ummah
were of being amongst the hypocrites. So, fear is needed in
order to protect my faith.

As Ibn al-Qayyim (may Allah have mercy on him) said,
*"The more faith and knowledge a person has, the more he will fear
that he may be among this class of people (hypocrites)."*

The more we fear hypocrisy, the more we can protect
our faith and the more we can hope to be amongst those
who receive His glad tidings as mentioned in verse 25 of
Surah Al-Baqarah:

وَبَشِّرِ ٱلَّذِينَ ءَامَنُوا۟ وَعَمِلُوا۟ ٱلصَّٰلِحَٰتِ أَنَّ لَهُمْ جَنَّٰتٍ تَجْرِى مِن تَحْتِهَا ٱلْأَنْهَٰرُ ۖ كُلَّمَا رُزِقُوا۟ مِنْهَا مِن ثَمَرَةٍ رِّزْقًا ۙ قَالُوا۟ هَٰذَا ٱلَّذِى رُزِقْنَا مِن قَبْلُ ۖ وَأُتُوا۟ بِهِۦ مُتَشَٰبِهًا ۖ وَلَهُمْ فِيهَآ أَزْوَٰجٌ مُّطَهَّرَةٌ ۖ وَهُمْ فِيهَا خَٰلِدُونَ ﴿٢٥﴾

"And give glad tidings to those who believe and do righteous deeds that they will have gardens [in Paradise] beneath which rivers flow. Whenever they are provided with a provision of fruit therefrom, they will say, 'This is what we were provided with before.' And it is given to them in likeness. And they will have therein purified spouses, and they will abide therein eternally."

A balance of fear and hope is something we should always strive for with the help of Allah, *subhaanahu wa ta'alaa (Glorified and High is He.)*

15

Yaa Rabb, Cleanse My Heart
by Hajara Salihu

وَإِذَا لَقُواْ ٱلَّذِينَ ءَامَنُواْ قَالُوٓاْ ءَامَنَّا وَإِذَا خَلَوْاْ إِلَىٰ شَيَـٰطِينِهِمْ قَالُوٓاْ إِنَّا مَعَكُمْ إِنَّمَا نَحْنُ مُسْتَهْزِءُونَ ﴿١٤﴾

ٱللَّهُ يَسْتَهْزِئُ بِهِمْ وَيَمُدُّهُمْ فِى طُغْيَـٰنِهِمْ يَعْمَهُونَ ﴿١٥﴾

أُوْلَـٰئِكَ ٱلَّذِينَ ٱشْتَرَوُاْ ٱلضَّلَـٰلَةَ بِٱلْهُدَىٰ فَمَا رَبِحَت تِّجَـٰرَتُهُمْ وَمَا كَانُواْ مُهْتَدِينَ ﴿١٦﴾

"And when they meet those who believe, they say, 'We believe.' But when they are alone with their evil ones, they say, 'Indeed, we are with you; we were only mockers.' [But] Allah mocks them and prolongs them in their transgression [while] they wander blindly. Those are the ones who have purchased error [in exchange] for guidance, so their transaction has brought no profit, nor were they guided."
—*Al-Baqarah*, 14-16

It goes without saying that one has to be intentional when choosing their company.

It is worthy to note that one is not above falling into *nifaaq* (hypocrisy) or *ghuroor* (self-deception). Hence, we have to constantly seek the guidance of Allah and beg Allah to purify our intentions.

Allah stated that He will punish the hypocrites for their mockery. This is enough for us to learn that all of our deeds never go unrecorded.

Why then do we prefer misguidance?

Allah, Who is ever Merciful and Gracious, gives the news of glad tidings to the believers of gardens in Paradise beneath which rivers flow and the provisions therein, as a means to remind the believers that the life of this world is only but delusion.

Yaa Rabb, cleanse my heart from the filth of my sins, from nifaaq and ghuroor, preserve my eeman and keep me in the company of those who constantly remind me of You!

16

Hypocrisy Taunts Me
by Umm Jameelah

وَمِنَ ٱلنَّاسِ مَن يَقُولُ ءَامَنَّا بِٱللَّهِ وَبِٱلْيَوْمِ ٱلْأَخِرِ وَمَا هُم بِمُؤْمِنِينَ ﴿٨﴾

يُخَٰدِعُونَ ٱللَّهَ وَٱلَّذِينَ ءَامَنُوا۟ وَمَا يَخْدَعُونَ إِلَّآ أَنفُسَهُمْ وَمَا يَشْعُرُونَ ﴿٩﴾

فِى قُلُوبِهِم مَّرَضٌ فَزَادَهُمُ ٱللَّهُ مَرَضًا وَلَهُمْ عَذَابٌ أَلِيمٌ بِمَا كَانُوا۟ يَكْذِبُونَ ﴿١٠﴾

"And of the people are some who say, 'We believe in Allah and the Last Day,' but they are not [really] believers. They [think to] deceive Allah and those who believe, but they deceive not except themselves and perceive [it] not. In their hearts is disease, so Allah has increased their disease; and for them is a painful punishment because they [habitually] used to lie."
—*Al-Baqarah, 2:8-10*

The issue here is that wrong is wrong, and I acknowledge that. But how to stop?

You see, it's not as bad as…

Wait, is that rationalizing?

It really could be worse, but I will be the first to admit that watching certain videos when I could be reading or listening to something beneficial for my thirsty soul is absolutely wrong, and I'd be delusional to rationalize a bit of it.

In the midst of writing, I even had to check myself. Time is heavy, and since becoming a mom and needing those minutes (LITERALLY MINUTES) to myself, I decide to catch up on all the YouTube videos I love to watch.

There's nothing wrong with leisure, but I can literally feel my soul leaking *emaan*. And I am forever thirsty. It's wrong, wrong, wrong—and to know the issue you have and do zilch to correct it… *O Allah, help me. I need you! Ameen.*

O Nifaaq, it's not permissible, but I feel like you're my second husband. Who taunts me. Whose only goal is to stop me from wanting to change.

Paralyzed at the intersection of action and good deeds, and pure at heart towards Allah and Islam as a whole.

Literally every day, hypocrisy taunts me. Now I can't press the gas. *O Allah, help me. I need to move!*

I'm trying but I can do better, Allah willing. I can do it. It's the reason I signed up for courses. To get back to my studies. To rectify my heart. My thirsty, rusted, hypocritical heart. I need my Islam. I hate hypocrisy.

Allah, I need you.

Dear reader, let this not be a de-motivator. Let it be a motivation to be better than the writer.

PART THREE
Sincerity

17

Finding Myself
by Umm Zakiyyah

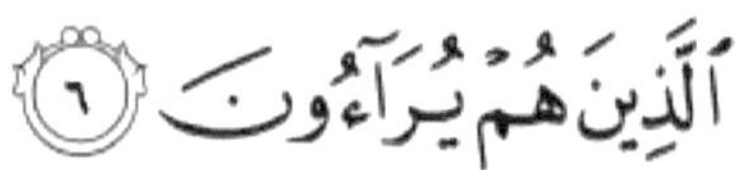

"[So, woe to the worshippers...]
Those who do good deeds only to be seen [of men]."
—Al-Maa'oon, (107:6)

I'm reminded of one of the most difficult challenges I faced when I decided to not only hold on to my faith but to also stay connected to the Muslim community, and then teach Qur'an:

Being comfortable with just being me, without filtering my "human parts" through the lens of what so many people were saying a "Qur'an teacher" should look like and sound like.

I tried for years to fit into the "Qur'an student/teacher prototype" but I just ended up feeling like I was doing these "good things" just to be liked and approved of by the "real" people of the Qur'an (i.e. my Arabic-speaking teachers and their dedicated American students who mimicked them in everything from speech patterns to food choices to clothing).

So, I was asked to change how I spoke, how I walked, how I dressed, and even how I wrote books—because many felt that my writing fiction stories and novels was "inappropriate" for a person of the Qur'an. It didn't matter that my books were inspiring people to become Muslim, by the mercy of Allah. All that mattered was that some "important religious people" felt uncomfortable with me being involved in both Islamic teaching and "entertainment."

A couple of years ago, I lost the friendship of a beloved Qur'an teacher after I drew a boundary and let her know that I was not going to change the way I spoke (which she felt was "too emotional" because I tend to get choked up and my voice inflection rises when I'm speaking my heart).

And this boundary deeply offended her.

She was used to the "Baiyinah" who listened to her constant criticism and just calmly accepted that I was the one who needed to change. But I told her she's trying to shape me into a "good Arab woman" instead of just hearing my heart and letting me be *me*, a striving Muslim woman who is culturally an American.

"I'm not going to change how I speak," I told her. "Allah gave me my voice, and unless I'm saying something displeasing to Him, I won't silence it anymore."

We haven't spoken in almost two years. This was a side of me she couldn't handle or accept.

I wish I could say I don't care and I'm better off without her. But the truth is, I miss her and wish we could've worked through this. I keep her in my *du'aa*.

And till today, I do sometimes wonder if I could do a better job at speaking my heart, because it so often offends people. And I don't like hurting others, especially when I'm intending to just share my heart and connect with them.

"You need to understand that your voice itself is intimidating," a loved one told me once. "Even if you don't mean to, the way you speak is difficult to handle."

But how do you go about changing your voice?

I honestly don't know.

So, I just make *du'aa* to Allah to help me find a balance between being myself and being beloved by Him. Because my emotional health can no longer handle trying to be a "good Muslim woman" in ways that make everyone else happy, but not myself.

18

Who Is Allah? I Wondered
by Umm Katheer

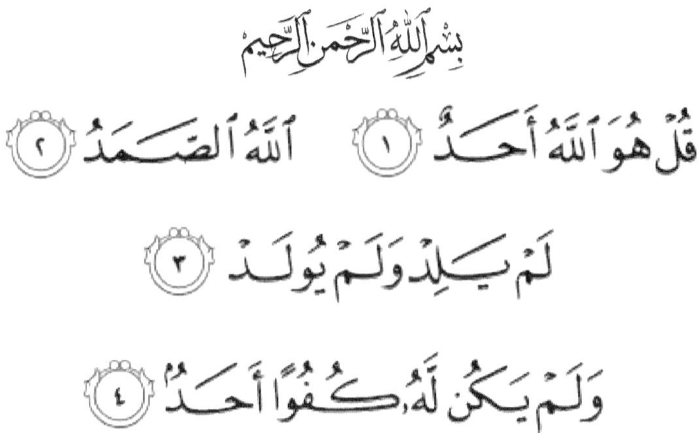

"*Say, 'He is Allah, [the] One and Only. Allah, the Eternal Refuge. He begets not, nor was He begotten. And there is none like unto Him.'*"
—*Al-Ikhlaas*, 112:1-4

Whenever I recite or think about *Suratul-Ikhlaas* (Surah 112), the first *ayah* reminds me of how much I yearned to know exactly who Allah is. I was about five years old when we had our first conversations. He comforted me at night. I felt His presence and knew He was real before I had any knowledge of His other characteristics.

No one made me believe in Him.

At about eleven years old, I remember how when I was in the masjid and the brother said, " قُلْ/Qul (Say)," and when he got to the end of that first statement, I recall his index finger pointing up to the sky. I didn't know any Arabic at the time, but the tone of the words told me these words have to be paid deep, serious attention to.

He kept telling me about *Tawheed*, the Oneness of Allah. So simple, yet so profound at the same time. My heart and mind were screaming out, "I knew it!"

I felt as though I'd been just told about the biggest secret in the world and as if I had a lifetime of treasures inside of my soul.

He confirmed something I always felt while I was going to church as a young child. I understood why my heart had felt cold and hard when the leaders there spoke about "three." I knew He wasn't three. He's One. The Only One, Unique. Nothing like us. *Alhamdulillah*. And I can talk to Him whenever I want.

I took my *shahaadah* soon after that day.

19

Misguidance Looked Beautiful to Him
by Amatullah bint Abdullah

وَعَادًا وَثَمُودَاْ وَقَد تَّبَيَّنَ لَكُم مِّن مَّسَـٰكِنِهِمَّ وَزَيَّنَ لَهُمُ الشَّيْطَـٰنُ أَعْمَـٰلَهُمْ فَصَدَّهُمْ عَنِ السَّبِيلِ وَكَانُواْ مُسْتَبْصِرِينَ ﴿٣٨﴾

"…Shaytaan beautified their deeds [and made them fair-seeming] to them, and turned them away from the [right] Path, though they were gifted with intelligence and skill."
—*Al-'Ankaboot*, 29:38

I wondered whether or not to share this reflection due to the personal nature of the story, but thought that perhaps it may be beneficial to our readers, *inshaaAllah*.

When I reflected on how misguidance could have been presented in my life to look beautiful, I honestly could not think of any instances. That's not to say I've never been misguided, but that I cannot recall a time I thought of it as something good or beautiful.

But I have witnessed it happen to someone I loved. When I married him, I thought he would help keep me steadfast and that he was the *qawwaam* I needed to stay strong in the *deen*. But our marriage was tested in ways I never imagined, and I found myself having to carry both myself and him to stay on the path. Suddenly, "self-care" trumped everything.

I won't go into details of how exactly he chose "self-care" over "soul-care," for my wish to be veiled on the Day of Judgment matters more to me than teaching others lessons. But what I've seen happen to my husband has been the greatest test of my life, because if I allowed myself, I could have easily succumbed to the ease and justification of "taking care of myself" over pleasing Allah *subhaanahu wa ta'alaa (Glorified and High is He)*.

Though, I want to be clear. Taking care of one's self and taking care of one's soul are not mutually exclusive. It's possible to care for one without compromising the other.

To our cherished readers: This is not to say that I judge him or believe myself to be better than him in any way. I know that without the mercy of Allah, I could easily be in his shoes. In fact, many times, I've considered it myself, but was afraid of closing my eyes to sleep one night and waking up shrouded in my dark grave. Every day that I open my eyes and am given another chance to repent, I consider it a gift.

I ask Allah to help keep me steadfast, keep me aware of how misguidance can be beautified by the Shaytaan, and to keep me far away from it. I pray that Allah beautifies for us all the sweetness of *emaan*, and creates within us a deep dislike for disbelief, transgression, and disobedience. And may Allah make us of the Guided Ones.

20

Share a Special Moment with Me
by Kameelah Muslimah Kareem

هُوَ ٱلَّذِى خَلَقَ ٱلسَّمَٰوَٰتِ وَٱلْأَرْضَ فِى سِتَّةِ أَيَّامٍ ثُمَّ ٱسْتَوَىٰ عَلَى ٱلْعَرْشِ يَعْلَمُ مَا يَلِجُ فِى ٱلْأَرْضِ وَمَا يَخْرُجُ مِنْهَا وَمَا يَنزِلُ مِنَ ٱلسَّمَآءِ وَمَا يَعْرُجُ فِيهَا وَهُوَ مَعَكُمْ أَيْنَ مَا كُنتُمْ وَٱللَّهُ بِمَا تَعْمَلُونَ بَصِيرٌ ﴿٤﴾

لَّهُ مُلْكُ ٱلسَّمَٰوَٰتِ وَٱلْأَرْضِ وَإِلَى ٱللَّهِ تُرْجَعُ ٱلْأُمُورُ ﴿٥﴾

يُولِجُ ٱلَّيْلَ فِى ٱلنَّهَارِ وَيُولِجُ ٱلنَّهَارَ فِى ٱلَّيْلِ وَهُوَ عَلِيمٌ بِذَاتِ ٱلصُّدُورِ ﴿٦﴾

"It is He who created the heavens and earth in six days and then established Himself above the Throne. He knows what penetrates into the earth and what emerges from it and what descends from the heaven and what ascends therein; and He is with you wherever you are. And Allah, of what you do, is Seeing. His is the dominion of the heavens and earth. And to Allah are returned [all] matters. He causes the night to enter the day and causes the day to enter the night, and He is Knowing of that within the breasts."
—*Al-Hadeed, 57:4-6*

Dedicated to you and I, my loves

*B*ismillaahir-Rahmanir-Raheem: I'll share with you something I've learned… something very special and close to my heart. Some time ago, in my journeys through life, I've acquired some precious knowledge, and remember, sharing knowledge is always love.

So, my dearest seekers of love and knowledge, what have I experienced? I've learned personally that tears and sadness are necessary. Sadness is a natural feeling that we need to allow ourselves to experience, *maashaAllah*. It's a feeling I no longer run from. I've also learned that there is something very special behind the determined, sorrowful tears. Something that surprisingly brings me moments of true, unexpected, blessed happiness, *alhamdulillah*.

What is buried inside us beneath the troubled, heart-wrenching tears? Within the aching pain we so compassionately try to escape? Honestly, I question if I'd even know had I not experienced the long-term effects of striving for *sabr*. The long-term effects of my *nafs*, *qalb*, and *rooh* striving closely and purposefully together to overcome a battle within myself and my emotional and spiritual mind. Sometimes I win and sometimes I lose, *Allahu 'alim (Allah knows best)*.

Still trust, my loves, just believe me, when you win that battle, when you gain victory over your *nafs*, do you know the incredible feeling? Pure hope and reliance on Allah comforted with His love and Mercy is a feeling I've experienced beneath this temporary shedding of the beautiful tear for His sake.

There are times we pass the most difficult, unexpected tests with *sabr* and even with all the remaining scars and wounds, there is a true, complete happiness in connecting with your Creator, Allah *subhaanahu wa ta'alaa (Glorified and High is He!)* An unexplainable, at times, incomprehensive contentment and joy in realizing He really, truly was with you the entire time. The. Whole. Time. This is a lesson I pray to hold fast to in my own story, and may Allah grant us all a good and happy ever after, Ameen! Whatsoever that may be, He knows best!

Never, ever lose hope in the Mercy of Allah. He was with you then. He is with you always. The help of Allah is always near. Have patience, my loves. With hardship comes ease. With hardship comes ease. With pain, time, struggle, trials, and hardship comes promised, definite, gratifying, mysterious, and beautiful ease. Have *tawakkul*, have strength, have beautiful *sabr* my loves.

With love and hope,
for His sake (*fisabilillaah*),
KMK

21

The Opening Chapter of My Faith
by Aminah Hamidullah

"In the name of Allah, Most Gracious, Most Merciful. All praise is due to Allah, Lord of all the worlds. Most Gracious, Most Merciful. Master of the Day of Judgment. You alone do we worship, and from You alone do we seek help and aid. Show us the Straight Path, the path of those who have earned Your favor, not of those who have earned Your wrath, nor of those who have gone astray."
—*Al-Faatihah*, 1:1-7

When I think of the moment, so many years ago when I accepted Islam, I think of *Al-Faatihah*, the opening chapter of the Qur'an. Because truly, for me, it was this Surah that clarified for me the truth of Islam. That's why I consider it the opening chapter of my faith. Till today, I turn to *Al-Faatihah* as a means to keep me focused and help me through any spiritual confusion.

Unfortunately, there is so much misinformation about Islam today and so many misunderstandings of what our Creator is telling us. And, because there's so much I don't know and am still learning, I sometimes feel so overwhelmed. This happens sometimes when I'm listening to a lecture by a sheikh or an imam and I don't understand what is being taught, or I fear that what is being taught might not be correct, so I want to know what is correct in front of Allah.

But whenever I begin to feel confused or uncertain, I recite this prayer, inspired by the sixth *ayah* of *Al-Faatihah*: "[O Allah] guide me to the Right Path." And each time I make this prayer, *subhaanAllah*. Allah makes the truth clear for me.

Just like He made the truth clear for me when He guided me to Islam the first time.

I don't have the words to explain just how much *Al-Faatihah* meant to me as a new Muslim. But I can say this: One of the things I learned from studying the *tafseer* of *Al-Faatihah* is that one of its names is *Umm Al-Kitaab*, meaning the Mother of the Book. And just hearing that really soothed my heart.

After accepting Islam and being the only Muslim in my family, I would often feel really lonely and disheartened at times. But like a compassionate mother comforting me no matter what I was going through, the opening Surah of the Qur'an brought me solace, compassion, and direction.

And it still does till today.
All praise is due to the Allah, the Lord of all the worlds.

PART FOUR

Hope in Allah

22

Glad Tidings for Imperfect Souls
by Umm Zakiyyah

وَبَشِّرِ ٱلَّذِينَ ءَامَنُوا۟ وَعَمِلُوا۟ ٱلصَّٰلِحَٰتِ أَنَّ لَهُمْ جَنَّٰتٍ تَجْرِى مِن تَحْتِهَا ٱلْأَنْهَٰرُ ۖ كُلَّمَا رُزِقُوا۟ مِنْهَا مِن ثَمَرَةٍ رِّزْقًا ۙ قَالُوا۟ هَٰذَا ٱلَّذِى رُزِقْنَا مِن قَبْلُ ۖ وَأُتُوا۟ بِهِۦ مُتَشَٰبِهًا ۖ وَلَهُمْ فِيهَآ أَزْوَٰجٌ مُّطَهَّرَةٌ ۖ وَهُمْ فِيهَا خَٰلِدُونَ ﴿٢٥﴾

"And give glad tidings to those who believe and do righteous deeds that they will have gardens [in Paradise] beneath which rivers flow. Whenever they are provided with a provision of fruit therefrom, they will say, 'This is what we were provided with before.' And it is given to them in likeness. And they will have therein purified spouses, and they will abide therein eternally."
—Al-Baqarah, 2:45

It wasn't something I really considered before this moment, at least not that I recall. Before this difficult time in my life—wherein I was striving so hard to hold on to my *emaan*—so much of my faith had been about being as close to perfect as humanly possible.

I not only stayed away from sins. I stayed away from anything that could even *possibly* be labeled "doubtful"—just to be safe—even if I myself wasn't truly convinced that it was *haraam*.

But I was mentally and emotionally exhausted. And I feared I didn't have the strength to go on like this. I felt my willpower breaking, my *emaan* weakening, and the wounding on my soul deepening.

Deep inside, I knew something had to give. I needed to find a way to balance my spiritual soul-care with my worldly self-care such that neither suffered.

But what if I make a mistake? What if I do something wrong? What if I end up in Hellfire?

It was while reading this *ayah* of the Qur'an that I got my answer, and my heart was comforted: "*And give glad tidings to those who believe and do righteous deeds that they will have gardens [in Paradise]…*"

Allah didn't say, "And give glad tidings to those who believe and never make a mistake or fall into sin." He commanded that the glad tidings of Paradise be given to those who fit into only two categories:

(1) They have *emaan*.

(2) They are doing good deeds.

And in other parts of the Qur'an, Allah let us know over and over that these people will be granted His forgiveness and mercy.

It was then that I realized that I was overlooking the obvious all along, hence the inspiration behind this personal reminder to my restless soul: *Allah promises forgiveness and mercy to those who believe. If we were meant to be perfect and sinless, then tell me, dear soul, exactly what is He forgiving us for?*

23

He Is Most Gracious, Most Merciful
by Sabah Hassan Abdillahi

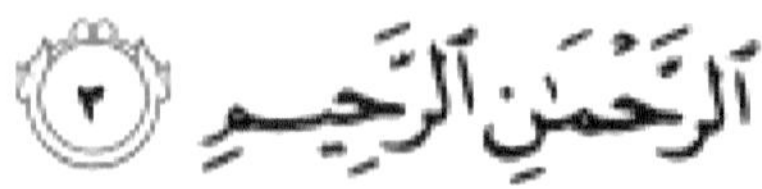

"[He is] Ar-Rahmaan, Ar-Raheem"
—Al-Faatihah, 1:3

Only with the permission of Allah, I write and document my personal reflection.

The way these two names stand alone in one verse, Ar-Rahmaan and Ar-Raheem, is enough to just pause and ponder on.

These two beautiful names and attributes of Allah—"The Most Merciful, The Bestower of Mercy"—give me immense hope in Allah's mercy. His mercy encompasses everything that exists, and He is more merciful than a mother is to her child.

No matter what difficulty I am going through, I should have hope, because Ar-Rahmaan, Ar-Raheem, is aware of my situation. I just need to do my part to be fully enclosed in His mercy. I have to:

1. Worship Him.
2. Keep my tongue wet with His *dhikr* and *istighfaar.* As the Qur'an says [what has been translated to

mean]: "*Should you not have asked forgiveness of Allah, so that you may receive mercy?*" (*An-Naml*, 27:46)

3. Show mercy to his creation, humans and animals. As "Verily, Allah's mercy is [always] near to the doers of good" (*Al-A'raaf*, 7:56).
4. Continue to make *du'aa*. For I will only enter Jannah by his mercy because no matter how many good deeds I do, it will never reach or catch up to the blessing He has bestowed on me.

24

The Answer Is in the Book, Al-Qur'an
by Kathryn Holmes-Adamu

إِنَّ فِى خَلْقِ ٱلسَّمَٰوَٰتِ وَٱلْأَرْضِ وَٱخْتِلَٰفِ ٱلَّيْلِ وَٱلنَّهَارِ لَءَايَٰتٍ لِّأُو۟لِى ٱلْأَلْبَٰبِ ﴿١٩٠﴾

ٱلَّذِينَ يَذْكُرُونَ ٱللَّهَ قِيَٰمًا وَقُعُودًا وَعَلَىٰ جُنُوبِهِمْ وَيَتَفَكَّرُونَ فِى خَلْقِ ٱلسَّمَٰوَٰتِ وَٱلْأَرْضِ رَبَّنَا مَا خَلَقْتَ هَٰذَا بَٰطِلًا سُبْحَٰنَكَ فَقِنَا عَذَابَ ٱلنَّارِ ﴿١٩١﴾

"Indeed, in the creation of the heavens and the earth and the alternation of the night and the day are signs for those of understanding. Who remember Allah while standing or sitting or [lying] on their sides and give thought to the creation of the heavens and the earth, [saying], 'Our Lord, You did not create this aimlessly. Exalted are You [above such a thing]. So, protect us from the punishment of the Fire!'"
—*Ali 'Imraan*, 3:190-191

It has always been so near
The answers for all of my fears

What book did I not read
As I lay crying in my bed

Year in, and year out

Problems old and new, what's the best way for a solution
to go about?

The pattern of solving them unchanged
Whether online, from a library, my method still the same

I finally grab my copy of THE BLESSED book up high on
my shelf
I brush off the dust, and tell myself, "Maybe it will help"

In His Book, HE speaks to me in a language so easy to
understand
The signs are everywhere in front of me to see, in His
blessed land

His emphasis in these *ayaat* focusing on HIS signs that
alternate in their own course
The times fixed and LIMITED, an example for me to
follow as I read the next verse

He instructs me to remember Him in so many ways
Whether I'm standing, sitting or lying down, while giving
Him praise

He didn't leave me to myself, as I navigate my woes
He left me a *du'aa* for succor and strength that will always
remind me of HIS goals

So as I go forward, from this day to the next,
Let me contemplate upon the succession of HIS signs,
patiently bearing my woes seeking HIS protection from the
fiery blast

25

I Am My Passion Project
by Layla Graham

وَٱبْتَغِ فِيمَآ ءَاتَىٰكَ ٱللَّهُ ٱلدَّارَ ٱلْءَاخِرَةَ وَلَا تَنسَ نَصِيبَكَ مِنَ ٱلدُّنْيَا وَأَحْسِن كَمَآ أَحْسَنَ ٱللَّهُ إِلَيْكَ وَلَا تَبْغِ ٱلْفَسَادَ فِي ٱلْأَرْضِ إِنَّ ٱللَّهَ لَا يُحِبُّ ٱلْمُفْسِدِينَ ۝

"But seek, through that which Allah has given you, the home of the Hereafter; and [yet], do not forget your share of the world. And do good as Allah has done good to you. And desire not corruption in the land. Indeed, Allah does not like corrupters."
—Al-Qasas, 28:77

*A*llah *knows me better than I know myself.*
This was my main thought through this week's course and the particular *ayah* that Ustadha decided to focus on this time. I took a look at the title of this week's course, "You Can Be Successful, Joyful and Spiritually Healthy" and made assumptions about what would be said.

"Sure," I told myself, "I know we can pair spiritual health and *dunya* happiness."

I should've known better, though. Our dear Umm Zakiyyah is nothing if not genuine in her desire to serve us truths that would inspire deep reflection. (*May Allah bless her. Ameen.*)

As the lesson went by, I found myself panicking inwardly. No longer could I hide behind the comfort of journal entries and incoherent reflections scribbled between the pages.

I am being asked to seek joy in *halaal* passion projects or hobbies at a time when I feel so incredibly grief-stricken and fatigued. I received this assignment only twenty-four hours before I finally decided to end my marriage.

I chose me. I am my own passion project.

And it is the most difficult thing that I've ever had to do; the most heart wrenching decision made only after many months of contemplation, and many hours of consulting one-on-one with Allah.

How could a divorce be something that brings me joy, and allows me to take my part of this world?

I don't know the answer to that just yet, as I am still very raw with the reality of this loss, but I know in my heart that this is what has been prescribed for me.

Allah says in this *ayah*: *"And do good as Allah has done good to you."* In the midst of my grief over the end of my marriage, I have been given opportunities to do good for myself and for others, all praise belongs to the Almighty. This brings me joy. This is a balm on my heart. This allows me to see the loveliness in this world.

I am so grateful for the gift we have in the Salaah of *Istikhaarah* and for being the slave of a Lord who listens 24 hours a day, 7 days a week, 365 days a year. I am forever humbled by how insignificant I am in comparison to other creations of His, and yet, still significant to The Creator Himself.

This shakes me to my core every time I stand to pray *Istikhaarah*, and ask Allah to destine goodness for me, and ward off anything that would harm me. What a magnificent gift.

I don't know what is in store for me in this *dunya*, but I do plan on taking my part of it, as has been ordered of me by my Rabb. I am looking forward to meeting Him, but ask Allah not to part my soul from my body unless He is pleased with me.

This entry is dedicated to my amazing teacher, mentor, and sister in Islam, Baiyinah Umm Zakiyyah. You are an amazing soul. May Allah reward you the best of rewards.

26

A Compassionate Note to Self
by Umm Maryam

هُوَ ٱللَّهُ ٱلَّذِى لَآ إِلَـٰهَ إِلَّا هُوَ ٱلْمَلِكُ ٱلْقُدُّوسُ ٱلسَّلَـٰمُ ٱلْمُؤْمِنُ ٱلْمُهَيْمِنُ ٱلْعَزِيزُ ٱلْجَبَّارُ ٱلْمُتَكَبِّرُ ۚ سُبْحَـٰنَ ٱللَّهِ عَمَّا يُشْرِكُونَ ﴿٢٣﴾

"He is Allah, other than whom none has the right to be worshipped, Knower of the unseen and the seen. He is the Most Gracious, the Most Merciful. He is Allah—there is no god but He—the Sovereign, the Pure, the Perfection, the Bestower of Faith, the Overseer, the Exalted in Might, the Compeller, the Superior. Exalted is Allah above whatever they associate with Him."
—Al-Hashr, 59:23

Dear Self,

You need to know and understand there is no deity other than Allah, and you cannot take deities like money, career, love, relationships as your god. Allah is Al-Malik, the King of the kings, and you get to talk to Him without making any prior appointments, at any time of the day, in any clothes that you are wearing, in any place that you are in, without any protocols. You should take this amazing opportunity and stand in your *fard* (obligatory) Salaah with utmost *khushoo'*.

Allah is Al-Quddus, the Pure, and you need to take care of your hygiene, your children's cleanliness, your home, etc. This is about physical cleanliness.

You need to keep your heart clean by not getting jealous even in the least bit. Your tongue should be clean of *gheebah*, *nameemah* and lying. Your mind should be clean of evil thoughts—no more fantasizing men celebs, no more *zina*!

Allah is As-Salaam, the Perfect, and you need to do everything that you lay your hands on to near perfection. You should give 100% to anything that you put your mind to and *inshaAllah*, with Allah's help, you will achieve the best even though it won't be perfect...it gotta be near perfect.

Allah is Al-Mu'min, the Grantor of security. As a good Muslim, everybody that you interact with should be granted security from your tongue and hands. Your speech should be kind so as not to hurt others. Your neighbors should be secure from you and your family's presence. Your friends and family should be secured by your words. If you promise to do something, then you must not bail out, and no matter what, you should always show up.

Why would you fear when you know Allah is Al-Muhaymin? He watches over His creatures. When you know He guards you against harm and provides sustenance for you. If you feel the restriction of *rizq*, then you should increase your *adhkaar*. The Prophet Muhammad (peace and blessings be upon him) was quoted as saying, "Call on Allah being certain that He will answer you" Sunan al-Tirmidhī 3479, *hasan*).

You should seek honour and power only from Al-Azeez. He is the One who can make anything happen. So you should work to seek His pleasure and be confident He will help you on the path. You should not shrink from practicing Islam in its totality in your community filled with liberals. Your *'izzah* (honor) is in Islam.

Call out on Al-Jabbar to fix all the broken relationships, broken hearts and all the broken situations. Live your life such that you reach people with brokenness with the help of Al-Jabbar to help fix their brokenness.

Every time you make fun of others or you laugh at them, remind yourself that it is because you think of yourself as better and because you have pride. Never be arrogant. Don't misuse your privilege. To Allah belongs the absolute pride. He is Al-Mutakabbir.

27

O Allah, I Have Wronged My Soul
by Amatullah bint Abdullah

ٱلَّذِينَ يُنفِقُونَ فِى ٱلسَّرَّآءِ وَٱلضَّرَّآءِ وَٱلْكَـٰظِمِينَ ٱلْغَيْظَ وَٱلْعَافِينَ عَنِ ٱلنَّاسِ ۗ وَٱللَّهُ يُحِبُّ ٱلْمُحْسِنِينَ ﴿١٣٤﴾

وَٱلَّذِينَ إِذَا فَعَلُوا۟ فَـٰحِشَةً أَوْ ظَلَمُوٓا۟ أَنفُسَهُمْ ذَكَرُوا۟ ٱللَّهَ فَٱسْتَغْفَرُوا۟ لِذُنُوبِهِمْ وَمَن يَغْفِرُ ٱلذُّنُوبَ إِلَّا ٱللَّهُ وَلَمْ يُصِرُّوا۟ عَلَىٰ مَا فَعَلُوا۟ وَهُمْ يَعْلَمُونَ ﴿١٣٥﴾

أُو۟لَـٰٓئِكَ جَزَآؤُهُم مَّغْفِرَةٌ مِّن رَّبِّهِمْ وَجَنَّـٰتٌ تَجْرِى مِن تَحْتِهَا ٱلْأَنْهَـٰرُ خَـٰلِدِينَ فِيهَا ۚ وَنِعْمَ أَجْرُ ٱلْعَـٰمِلِينَ ﴿١٣٦﴾

"Who spend [in the cause of Allah] during ease and hardship and who restrain anger and who pardon the people - and Allah loves the doers of good; And those who, when they commit a faahishah (illicit sexual act or immorality) or wrong themselves [by transgression], remember Allah and seek forgiveness for their sins - and who can forgive sins except Allah? And [who] do not persist in what they have done while they know. hose - their reward is forgiveness from their Lord and gardens beneath which rivers flow [in Paradise], wherein they will abide eternally; and excellent is the reward of the [righteous] workers."
—*Ali 'Imraan, 3:134-136*

Today's session had me weeping tears I didn't even know I had in me. To be fair, I cry almost every week, but this time I had to keep checking to make sure my microphone was on mute so Ustadha and the others didn't hear me hiccupping with sobs. These *ayaat*... How do I even articulate how much they mean to me personally?

I remember the very first time I studied these *ayaat* in depth. I was in middle school, and it was part of a school assignment. I remember thinking, *These traits don't seem very difficult to embody; being charitable, controlling one's anger, forgiving people, and staying away from prohibited sexual acts doesn't sound hard at all.*

Twelve-year-old me, you had no clue, girl.

The way our *dunya* has been shaped by people has made it outrageously difficult not only to do good, charitable things, but to refrain from sinning as well. I cringe when I recall the things I've said in anger. I look back at the things I previously thought to be unforgivable and wonder why I judged so harshly.

With age comes wisdom, but also a sense of understanding the intricacies of the *fitan* (severe trials) of this world. The older I grow, the more appreciation I have for our righteous predecessors, and the more empathy and compassion I have for those who sometimes fall astray.

When I think about the times I've wronged myself (i.e. have sinned and disobeyed Allah), it brings tears to my eyes to remember and recite this *ayah*:

"And those who, when they commit a shameful act or wrong themselves, remember Allah, then, seek forgiveness for their sins. And who is there to forgive sins except Allah? And they do not persist in what they've done knowingly."

This, to me, is the ultimate verse of hope for us all. The Rasul ﷺ said, "Every son of Adam is a sinner, and the best of wrongdoers are those who repent" (Sunan al-Tirmidhī 2499, *sahih*). Sometimes, when I am in a funk from a particular sin I've committed and feel the heat of shame from disobeying Allah, I remember that perhaps I was destined to commit this sin so that I may be inclined to fall to the ground in repentance. This isn't to justify any sins that I've committed, but to say, *Alhamdulillaah*, I belong to a Lord that is the Most Merciful and Most Forgiving.

This *ayah* in Surah Ali 'Imraan also reminds me of one of my favorite sayings of our beloved Rasul ﷺ:

"By The One Whose Hand my soul is within, if you (all) did not sin, Allah would have done away with you, and would have brought forth a people who sinned, so that they may seek His forgiveness, and He would forgive them" (Sahih Muslim).

And I know our beloved Messenger ﷺ would not swear by Allah for something that wasn't serious. Our Rabb is Al-Kareem, Al-Wadood, As-Samee', and Al- Ghaffaar (the Most Generous, Most Compassionate and Loving, All-Hearing, and Ever-Forgiving). *May all who read this always be worthy of His forgiveness.*

28

The Test

by Rasheedah Adisa

ٱلَّذِينَ يَجْتَنِبُونَ كَبَـٰٓئِرَ ٱلْإِثْمِ وَٱلْفَوَٰحِشَ إِلَّا ٱللَّمَمَ إِنَّ رَبَّكَ وَٰسِعُ ٱلْمَغْفِرَةِ هُوَ أَعْلَمُ بِكُمْ إِذْ أَنشَأَكُم مِّنَ ٱلْأَرْضِ وَإِذْ أَنتُمْ أَجِنَّةٌ فِى بُطُونِ أُمَّهَـٰتِكُمْ فَلَا تُزَكُّوٓا۟ أَنفُسَكُمْ هُوَ أَعْلَمُ بِمَنِ ٱتَّقَىٰٓ ﴿٣٢﴾

"Those who avoid the major sins and immoralities, only [committing] slight ones. Indeed, your Lord is vast in forgiveness. He was most knowing of you when He produced you from the earth and when you were fetuses in the wombs of your mothers. So do not claim yourselves to be pure; He is most knowing of who fears Him."
—An-Najm, 53:32

Some time ago, I went through a tough test
It was the kind that left me dazed and confused
The kind that leaves one wondering where they'd missed it
And makes you call out to Him from the depths of your heart
Day in, Day out
Not able to see much else
Not able to understand much of it
Not able to do much else
Except to grasp onto Him with all the strength left

Not letting go
Because in those moments you finally realize
The only being worth attaching yourself to unconditionally
is Him - Your Lord
Everything else is indeed transient
And on some days, it got too much
On some days it felt too hard
On some days I had no strength left
And my Lord knew
So He reminded me
Every time I said the words, "I can't, Lord! I give up!"
He would say to me through His Qur'an:

"Those who avoid great sins and shameful deeds, only (falling into) small faults - verily thy Lord is ample in forgiveness. He knows you well when He brings you out of the earth, and when ye are hidden in your mother's wombs. Therefore, justify not yourselves. He knows best who it is that guards against evil."

And there was my solace.

29

How Merciful Is My Rabb!
by Hajara Salihu

وَإِذَا سَأَلَكَ عِبَادِى عَنِّى فَإِنِّى قَرِيبٌ أُجِيبُ دَعْوَةَ ٱلدَّاعِ إِذَا دَعَانِّ فَلْيَسْتَجِيبُوا۟ لِى وَلْيُؤْمِنُوا۟ بِى لَعَلَّهُمْ يَرْشُدُونَ ۝

"When My servants ask you concerning Me, I am indeed near. I listen to the prayer of every supplicant when he calls on Me. Let them also, with a will, listen to My call and believe in Me, that they may be guided aright."
—*Al-Baqarah*, 2:186

Indeed, Allah is free of need. And oh, how distant I've become from my Rabb while He is always with me. Always ready to respond to my unending needs.
Allah has taught me several means to draw near to Him, yet I fall short.
Still, when I ask, He gives.
When I seek refuge, He protects me.
He is never an absent One.
How merciful is my Rabb.

Yaa Rabb, I should have done more, but I didn't. So forgive me. Grant me the patience and perseverance to accept Your decree upon me, the wisdom to understand that when I feel my du'aa's are not

Indeed, there's always more with Allah.

30

Thank You, Allah
by Umm Maryam

"And obey Allah and the Messenger that you may obtain mercy."
—Ali 'Imraan, 3:132

O Allah! I admit my shortcomings to You, and I admit my sins to You.

Yaa 'Aleem, You are All-Knowing, You know everything about me. You know my deepest, darkest secrets and even my passing thoughts.

I took your ahkaam (rulings) lightly, Yaa Rauf. You warned me and I forgot the warning. I let myself free, seeking happiness and pleasure from this fleeting world.

I became blind in the illusion, and I fell and I fell hard!!

Hadn't it been for Your mercy, I would have fallen in the dark dungeon for I don't know how long...

Yaa Raheem! You showered Your immense mercy on me when I didn't deserve even a glance from You!

You picked me up, cradled me and nursed me and lifted my fragile
body and caressed it.

You made Arabic letters of the Qur'an the coolness of my eyes…
On days when my heart pounded hard, just looking at half a page of
the Qur'an, soothed my aching qalb so beautifully as if it wasn't in
pain a few moments ago.

Thank you, Allah, for sending me people who comforted me. The day
when I was all alone in my room longing for a companion. I lifted my
head from the sujood and my neighbour, a beautiful Muslimah was
right in the house!! (I accidentally left the door ajar)

O Allah, how I wish I'd have acted upon Ali 'Imraan (3:132) in my
life.

"And obey Allah and the Messenger that you may obtain mercy."

I didn't obey You and I disobeyed the Messenger (peace be upon him),
and I did what I thought I'd never do. I learnt the lesson, the hard
way and I resolve to never take any of your commands lightly. I think
I have the option? No, I don't!! I resolve to submit to Your will in its
totality. Yaa Rabb, make it easy for me.

Tasting the Sweetness of Emaan

"He has tasted the sweetness of emaan who is content with Allah as a Rabb, Islam as a deen, and Muhammad as a messenger."
—Prophet Muhammad, peace be upon him (Sahih Muslim)

31

Let Your Belief Split Seas
by Umm Zakiyyah

مَآ أَصَابَ مِن مُّصِيبَةٍ فِى ٱلْأَرْضِ وَلَا فِىٓ أَنفُسِكُمْ إِلَّا فِى كِتَٰبٍ مِّن قَبْلِ أَن نَّبْرَأَهَآ ۚ إِنَّ ذَٰلِكَ عَلَى ٱللَّهِ يَسِيرٌ ﴿٢٢﴾

"No calamity befalls the earth or in yourselves, but is inscribed in the Book of Decrees before We bring it into existence. Verily, that is easy for Allah."
—*Al-Hadeed, 57:22*

It was supposed to be like this, all of it. I don't know why I didn't see it before. Every moment of happiness and joy. Every moment of sadness and pain. Every moment of emotional and spiritual confusion. And every single trial of ease and hardship that has befallen the world around me—and within the depths of my very *nafs*.

Every single part of my life was carefully written in the Preserved Tablet before I was even a clot of flesh awaiting my soul in my mother's womb.

It's all merely a test, a trial. That is it. To see whether or not I will patiently persevere upon *sabr*, nourishing my soul and bettering my life. Even when all I can see in front of me is a sea of pain and confusion, which I feel certain will drown me. And even when I all I can see behind me is an army of wrongdoers, whom I feel certain will drive me to the point of drowning.

Did I not read in the Qur'an the story of Musa (Moses), peace be upon him? Did my heart not learn about the honorable Prophet and Messenger who stood amidst the Children of Israel with the Red Sea in front of him and the army of Pharaoh behind him?

When this calamity befell me in my emotional and spiritual life—as my All-Wise Rabb promised it would—my heart began to cry, *Indeed, I am going to be overtaken by this pain and confusion!*

In this moment of emotional pain and spiritual weakness, I became like the despairing Children of Israel who saw the army of Pharaoh behind them and the Red Sea in front them, as Allah describes in the Qur'an:

فَلَمَّا تَرَٰٓءَا ٱلْجَمْعَانِ قَالَ أَصْحَٰبُ مُوسَىٰٓ إِنَّا لَمُدْرَكُونَ ﴿٦١﴾

*"And when the two companies saw one another, the companions of
Moses said, 'Indeed, we are to be overtaken!'"*
(Ash-Shu'uraa, 26:61).

Yet Prophet Musa, who too saw in front of his eyes every reason to be overcome with despair, was a person of *taqwaa*. He believed in the *ghayb*, the unseen triumph that his Ever-Truthful Rabb had promised him. So, instead of fixating on the pain of his present reality, his heart focused on a more truthful and lasting reality—the promise of guidance from the One whose Words contain within them no doubt:

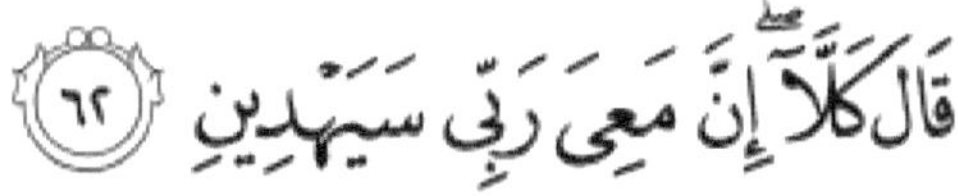

قَالَ كَلَّآ إِنَّ مَعِيَ رَبِّى سَيَهْدِينِ ﴿٦٢﴾

"[Moses] said, 'No! Indeed, with me is my Rabb; He will guide me'" (*Ash-Shu'uraa*, 26:62).

And as Al-Haqq continuously promises that He will do for His sincere and patient servants—the people of *taqwaa*—He came to the aid of His servant Prophet Musa and those who were with him, just when all seemed lost:

"Then We inspired to Moses, 'Strike with your staff the sea,' and it parted, and each portion was like a great towering mountain" (*Ash-Shu'uraa*, 26:63).

Thus, what was the outcome for Prophet Musa and those with him? Allah says:

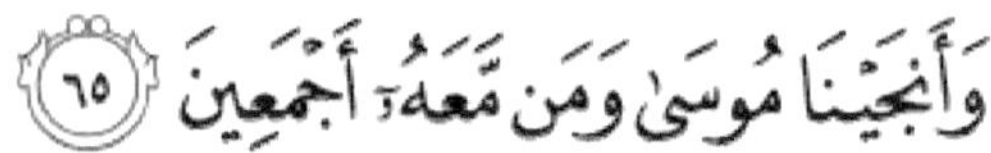

"And We saved Moses and those with him, all together" (*Ash-Shu'uraa*, 26:65).

Yet what was the outcome for the powerful army of wrongdoers who had enjoyed so much worldly pleasure, "honor" and victory over the "weak" believers before that moment?

"Then We drowned the others" (*Ash-Shu'uraa*, 26:66).

As my heart reflects on the powerful sign this holds in my own life, I am reminded of when my heart was awakened by the message of these Divine Words in a way it never had been before:

$$\text{الٓمٓ ۝}$$

$$\text{ذَٰلِكَ ٱلۡكِتَٰبُ لَا رَيۡبَ ۛ فِيهِ ۛ هُدٗى لِّلۡمُتَّقِينَ ۝}$$

$$\text{ٱلَّذِينَ يُؤۡمِنُونَ بِٱلۡغَيۡبِ وَيُقِيمُونَ ٱلصَّلَوٰةَ وَمِمَّا رَزَقۡنَٰهُمۡ يُنفِقُونَ ۝}$$

"Alif. Laam. Meem. This is the Book whereof there is no doubt, a guidance to those who are muttaqoon (people of taqwaa), who believe in the ghayb (unseen)…" (*Al-Baqarah*, 2:1-3).

Today, I pray I never lose my way (or myself) again. For I want to be of the believers who heed the signs that my Merciful Rabb continuously gives me—not of those who miss the entire point of the painful trials of life, simply because they are in the midst of those very trials of life.

But this is a path that requires *sabr*. And for the people of taqwaa, the path of *sabr* is not one of passive patience. It is one of active patience, as I remind myself in my journal:

Patient working, not patient waiting. This is what it means to have true tawakkul…Your trust in God is found in the continuous work you put into achieving what you're praying for—not in waiting around for God to just give it to you.

Regarding this I am reminded of the words of my brother in faith, Salih Ibn Yusuf, who posted this powerful reminder one day:

"Who said that after you ask God for a favour that you're supposed to wait for Him to provide? You have to work… WORK to reach the things in life that you want, but all in the meantime praying and giving thanks and acknowledgement to the One allowing you to pursue it… Be grateful and give thanks to the Most High. Let your belief split seas. God will not forsake you.' (@salihjohnwell via Instagram).

O Allah, Al-Kareem (the Most Generous)! We beg You to grant us beautiful sabr, sincere tawakkul, and a response to our every du'aa in way that is better than the best we could hope for or imagine!

About the Instructor and Founder of
Our Beautiful Qur'an Journey (Tadabbur)

Known for her soul-touching books and spiritual reflections on the Qur'an and emotional healing, Umm Zakiyyah is a world-renowned author and soul-care mentor.

Umm Zakiyyah studied Arabic, Qur'an, Islamic sciences, *'aqeedah*, and *tafseer* in America, Egypt, and Saudi Arabia for more than fifteen years. She currently teaches *tajweed* (rules of reciting Qur'an), *tafseer* (explanation of the meaning of the Qur'an), and *tadabbur* (deep reflections on the Qur'an) via uzhearthub.com.

Daughter of American converts to Islam, Umm Zakiyyah (also known by her birth name Ruby Moore and her "Muslim" name Baiyinah Siddeeq) is the internationally acclaimed, award-winning author of more than twenty-five books, including novels, short stories, and self-help. Her books are used in high schools and universities in the United States and worldwide, and her work has been translated into multiple languages. Her work has earned praise from writers, professors, and filmmakers. Her novel *His Other Wife* is now a short film.

Dr. Robert D. Crane, advisor to former US President Nixon, said of Umm Zakiyyah, "…no amount of training can bring a person without superb, natural talent to captivate the reader as she does and exert a permanent intellectual and emotional impact."

Professor K. Bryant of Howard University said of *If I Should Speak*, "The novel belongs to…a genre worthy of scholarly study."

Umm Zakiyyah has a BA degree in Elementary Education, an MA in English Language Learning, and Cambridge's CELTA (Certificate in English Language Teaching to Adults).

In 2020, she founded an online university to share the life lessons she learned on her emotional and spiritual healing journey. For information on UZ courses, including Our Beautiful Qur'an Journey (Tadabbur) go to **uzhearthub.com** and **uzuniversity.com**

Connect with Umm Zakiyyah online: **uzauthor.com**

Instagram: @uzauthor

Facebook: ummzakiyyahpage

YouTube: uzreflections

Special Thanks to Our Publishing Team

Executive Publisher: Umm Zakiyyah
She is an internationally acclaimed author, soul-care mentor, and founder of Our Beautiful Qur'an Journey at uzhearthub.com

Project Coordinator/Graphics: S. Majeedah
Affectionately called 'Sunny' for her bright and upbeat spirit, she chose Islam more than twenty years ago as a source of peace and a way out of a dark period in her life growing up in Baltimore. Today, she's a mom of five, CEO of a women's wellness center, outdoor enthusiast, and ongoing student of Qur'an and Tadabbur.

Assistant Project Coordinator: Layla Graham
Layla is an introverted millennial mother of two. She is *haafidhah* of Al-Qur'an and is also a Tajweed teacher. She is currently working towards two ijazahs *alhamdulillah*. Layla is also a certified early childhood Montessori guide, and an Al-Qa'idah An-Nooraniyah instructor. She runs a Qur'an blog on Instagram @alkitaab.almuneer and hopes to launch her business selling learning resources in the near future *bi'idhnillaah*: @primelearningresources on social media.

Editor-in-Chief: Aminah Hamidullah
She is the director and co-founder of Knowledge for Living, Inc., a non-profit 501C3, educational community organization. The organization serves as an educational organization providing training to low- and moderate-income communities.

She holds a BS Degree in Accounting and Finance with a minor in Economics and holds a Master's in Public Administration. She has completed post graduate studies in international finance with an emphasis in Islamic Banking.

Aminah has worked as Marketing Director for McDonald's Corporation, Recruiter and Advisor for the University of South Florida, VP for Bank of America, Financial Officer for SBA Business and Business Manager for the Muslim Academy of Central Florida.

Aminah has served as a member of the Mayor of Orlando Taskforce, and the Orlando police review board. She serves on the advisory board of Valencia College Peace & Justice.

She is an avid reader and is committed to a life of service.

Assistant Editor: Fatima Warshi

She is a psychology student aspiring to be a nurse. She chose this route because she has always loved asking individuals about their lives and the stories that made them into the people they are today. Psychology has given her insight and has aided her in understanding others.

Assistant Editor: Jasmin McClellan

Also known as Yasmin, she accepted Islam four years ago and is a twenty-five-year old mother of one. She is always looking for opportunities to better herself and her soul. She loves to learn, read, write occasionally, cook, and clean (and is a self-diagnosed as OCD in this). Overall, she's a fun, "goofy" Muslimah looking to learn to love her Lord, take care of herself and her family and ultimately be the best version of myself before returning to her Creator.

Images/Graphics Collector: Hajara Salihu

She is a lawyer based in Nigeria and is passionate about self-development and fostering interpersonal skills. She is the President/Co-founder of Al- Musaa'id foundation a non-profit organization working for the well-being and health of less privileged individuals. She seizes any opportunity she has to grow and better herself on the path of righteousness, fairness and honesty.

Also By Umm Zakiyyah

If I Should Speak
A Voice
Footsteps
Realities of Submission
Hearts We Lost
The Friendship Promise
Muslim Girl
His Other Wife
UZ Short Story Collection
The Test Paper (a children's book)
Pain. From the Journal of Umm Zakiyyah
Broken yet Faithful. From the Journal of Umm Zakiyyah
Faith. From the Journal of Umm Zakiyyah
Let's Talk About Sex and Muslim Love
Reverencing the Wombs That Broke You: A Daughter of Rape and Abuse Inspires Healing and Healthy Family
Prejudice Bones in My Body: Essays on Muslim Racism, Bigotry and Spiritual Abuse
And Then I Gave Up: Essays About Faith and Spiritual Crisis in Islam
I Almost Left Islam: How I Reclaimed My Faith
The Abuse of Forgiveness: Manipulation and Harm in the Name of Emotional Healing
even if. bits and pieces from the heart of Umm Zakiyyah
No One Taught Me the Human Side of Islam: The Muslim Hippie's Story of Living with Bipolar Disorder
He Asked About Islam
Alone, But In the Company of Your Lord
Come Back To Allah, Dear Soul: Salaah Coursebook
Dear Soul, It's Time: A Journey of Coming Back To Allah
I'm Divorced Now: Heartbreak and Healing
What Did You Expect? Lessons on Spiritual Honesty
Dear Struggling Soul: Affirmations for Spiritual Self-Compassion
Nurturing the Nafs: Emotional Honesty for the Female Soul
Learning Love: Self-Care Journal
Salaah Is a Blessing, Not a Burden
Your Lord Has Not Forgotten You: To the Non-Arab Learning Qur'an

Glossary of Common Arabic and Islamic Terms

adab: good manners; showing others humble respect; Islamic etiquette
alhamdulillah: "All praise belongs to Allah (God, the Creator) alone"
Allah: Arabic term for God; the only One who has the right to be
  worshipped
'aqeedah: foundational beliefs of the Islamic spiritual way of life
ayaat: plural form of *ayah*
ayah: verse from Qur'an or divine sign
'ayn: (literally "eye") used in reference to "the evil eye," which is often
  rooted in harmful envy or unhealthy admiration of someone devoid
  of mentioning Allah
bid'ah: sinful innovation in religion
bi'idhnillaah: "with the help of Allah (the Creator)"
da'wah: teaching others about Islam; inviting others to spiritual
  guidance
deen: spiritual way of life; religion
dhikr: sincere mention or remembrance of Allah (the Creator); message;
  reminder
dhulm: wrongdoing or oppression (of others or one's own soul)
du'aa: prayerful supplication; informal prayer
dunya: this worldly life as opposed to the Hereafter
'ebaadah: sincere worship, submission, and obedience to Allah alone
emaan: sincere faith; authentic spirituality; belief in Islam; *Tawheed*
faahishah: immorality, usually of a sexual nature
faasiq: evildoer; a person living in open sin or wrongdoing
fatwa: Islamic ruling or opinion given by a scholar
fisq: evil, corruption, or clear sin and wrongdoing
fitnah: (plural: *fitan*) difficult trial
fitrah: inherent inborn nature of every human soul to worship Allah
  alone and to live a spiritually and morally upright life
ghayb: unseen
gheebah: backbiting; saying anything about a fellow Muslim that if they
  were to hear it, they would dislike it
ghuroor: spiritual self-deception
halaal: divinely blessed or permissible
haraam: divinely forbidden or sinful
harf: a single Arabic letter (plural: *huroof*)
hasad: envy that is sinful and spiritually destructive
hasan: good; often used in reference to the rating of "good" regarding
  the strength of authenticity of a prophetic hadith

hijrah: migration from one land to another for the sake of your faith; moving from a place that harms the soul to a place that nourishes the soul

hikmah: literally "wisdom"; often used in reference to the divinely inspired prophetic wisdom

iftaar: the moment of breaking one's fast at sunset

ijmaa': unanimous agreement amongst the earliest Muslims and scholars

istighfaar: uttering supplications seeking Allah's forgiveness

Istikhaarah: prayer and supplication for making a decision about something

istislaam: spiritual surrender

jahiliyyah: pre-Islamic days of spiritual and moral ignorance before the prophetic assignment was given to Prophet Muhammad (peace be upon him); any mindset or life path that mirrors this spiritual and moral ignorance

Jahannam: Hellfire (also called Hell)

Jannah: Paradise (also called Heaven)

kaafir: disbeliever; any person who rejects a foundational part of Islam, who knowingly rejects a well-established principle or teaching of Islam, or who knowingly introduces or accepts any teaching that forbids what Allah allows or permits what Allah has forbidden regarding any matter wherein disagreement is not permitted

khaashi'oon: people who are defined by their *khushoo'*; those who are sincerely and humbly submissive in their worship and obedience to Allah

khula': female-initiation marriage dissolution

khushoo': sincerity and humility of the heart and soul; deep concentration in *Salaah* such that the heart is consistently spiritually nourished by its sincere and humble connection to its Creator in every part of prayer

kibr: sinful pride or pride that is spiritually harmful; looking down on others and rejecting the truth

kitaab: literally "book"; often used in reference to the Qur'an (i.e. the Book of Allah)

kufr: disbelief; spiritual blasphemy; any belief, speech or action that cancels one's *emaan*

Laa ilaaha illaa Allah: statement of *Tawheed* or declaration of faith that means, "Nothing has the right to be worshipped except Allah alone"

madhloom: one who has been wronged, oppressed, or suffered from *dhulm*

mahr: obligatory gift given to woman upon marriage; dowry

masjid: (plural: *masaajid*) the house of worship for the Muslim

nafs: inner-self or desires that are self-serving and spiritually harmful

nameemah: gossip or tale-carrying

naseehah: sincere advice offered to inspire soul-nourishment and life betterment in the one being advised

nikaah: Islamic marriage contract; often written and signed before the man and woman live together

qadar: divine decree; predestination

qalb: heart

qawwaam: the man's divinely assigned role of being the maintainer, provider, and protector of women in the home and society

Qiyaam ul-Layl: the blessed night prayer, prayed in last third of night

Rabb: another name for Allah that refers to His Lordship over creation; Creator, Owner and Manager of all that exists

rahmah: divine mercy

rak'ah: one unit of *Salaah* (formal prayer)

riba: usury

riyaa: insincerity; showing off; seeking the pleasure, admiration, reward, or attention of other than Allah

rizq: provision or wealth

ruqyaa': spiritual healing that includes reciting the Qur'an over someone and/or reciting *dhikr* and prayerful supplications for the purpose of healing illness or removing the effects of *'ayn* or *sihr* on someone

sabr: sincere patience; patiently persevering upon that which benefits one's life and soul, and patiently persevering in abstaining from that which harms one's life and the soul

sadaqah: voluntary, non-obligatory charity

sahih/saheeh: authentic; the highest grade of a hadith's authenticity

sajdah: prostrating the forehead on the floor in submission to Allah

Salaah: the five foundational prayers: *Fajr, Dhuhr, 'Asr, Maghrib,* and *'Ishaa'*; second pillar of Islam; formal prayer, whether optional or obligatory

sallallaahu'alayhi wa sallam: (ﷺ) prayers of peace and blessing upon the Prophet

shahaadah: formal declaration of faith that marks one's entry into Islam: "I bear witness that nothing has the right to be worshipped except Allah alone, and I bear witness that Muhammad is His slave and messenger"; sincere testimony of *Tawheed* recited repeatedly throughout a Muslim's life

Shaytaan: the devil; Satan

shirk: assigning divine attributes to creation or creation's attributes to the Creator

shukr: sincere gratefulness, thankfulness or gratitude

sihr: often referred to as "black magic": when someone works with the jinn to harm someone or get a specific outcome in this world

soorah/surah: (plural: *suwar*) divine chapter of the Qur'an

SubhaanAllah: statement of glorification of Allah: "Glory to Allah, and Exalted and High is He above any imperfection"

sujood: another term for *sajdah:* prostrating the forehead on the floor in submission to Allah

Sunnah: prophetic guidance or example; the life and teachings of Prophet Muhammad (peace and blessings be upon him)

Sunni: a description of Muslims who affiliate with understanding and living Islam based on the prophetic Sunnah

tafseer: authentic interpretation and spiritual explanation of the *ayaat* of Qur'an

tajweed: rules of reciting the Qur'an based on one or more of the seven authentic prophetic recitation styles

taqwaa: sincere God-consciousness and daily soul care that protects the heart from corruption and the soul from spiritual harm in the Hereafter

tawakkul: sincere trust in the wisdom and decisions of the Creator

tawbah: sincere repentance; turning one's life around as a form of seeking forgiveness for past sins and wrongdoing

Tawheed: Oneness of Allah; singling out the Creator alone in worship; authentic monotheism; sincere belief in the Oneness of Allah

tazkiyyatun-nafs: purification of the soul; spiritual nourishment that is attained through sincerity while fulfilling the required and optional acts of worship in Islam

'ulamaa: scholars; people of spiritual knowledge (plural of *'aalim*)

ummah: all Muslims from every generation; worldwide faith community

uswah: example or pattern to be followed by others

Witr: highly recommended prayer performed after *Ishaa'* or at the closing of *Qiyaam ul-Layl* and consists of three units of prayer (odd number)

wudhoo': ritual ablution that is done before *Salaah*

zakaah/zakaat: obligatory charity paid from one's wealth and given to the needy

zina: fornication or adultery

www.ingramcontent.com/pod-product-compliance
Lightning Source LLC
Chambersburg PA
CBHW020352160726

47987CB00022BA/2563